The Age of Exploration

Reader

Core Knowledge®

Copyright © 2017 Core Knowledge Foundation
www.coreknowledge.org

All Rights Reserved.

Core Knowledge®, Core Knowledge Curriculum Series™,
Core Knowledge History and Geography™ and CKHG™
are trademarks of the Core Knowledge Foundation.

Trademarks and trade names are shown in this book
strictly for illustrative and educational purposes and are
the property of their respective owners. References herein
should not be regarded as affecting the validity of said
trademarks and trade names.

Printed in Canada

ISBN: 978-1-68380-064-4

The Age of Exploration

Table of Contents

The Age of Exploration
Reader
Core Knowledge History and Geography™

Chapter 1
The Spice Islands

The Spice of Life History can be changed by many things. A battle, an election, an earthquake, or even a rainstorm can alter the course of events. But would you ever have thought that peppercorns and cinnamon sticks could lead to one of history's great developments? Because it can easily be argued that the United States exists today because **medieval** Europeans liked spicy food.

The Big Question
....
According to the author, how did the search for the Spice Islands change history?

Vocabulary
....
medieval, adj. relating to the Middle Ages in Europe

spice, n. a plant used to add flavor to food

Supermarkets today stock all sorts of **spices** that can be used to season or add flavor to different foods. In medieval Europe, however, people relied on spices not only to flavor their food, but also as a way to preserve it. Without refrigerators or other cold storage, medieval Europeans used spices to extend the time period during which meats and other foods could be stored and then safely eaten before turning rotten.

Spices such as cinnamon sticks and peppercorns were very valuable in medieval Europe.

In the Middle Ages, spices were hard to get. Pepper, cinnamon, ginger, cloves, and other seasonings were grown in faraway Asia. Getting the spices to Europe took a lot of time and effort. Distances were great, and travel back and forth was dangerous. As a result, spices were very expensive. Europe's desire for cheaper spices sparked the Age of European Exploration and its settlement of the Americas.

The Spice Islands

Different spices come from different places. Many of the most desirable spices come from the islands of present-day Indonesia. Indonesia is an **archipelago**, or chain of islands. It stretches from Southeast Asia's Malay Peninsula to the continent of Australia. This group, known as the

> **Vocabulary**
> ....
> **archipelago,** n. a chain of islands

Malay Archipelago, contains more than thirteen thousand islands. Some, like Sumatra and Java, are large. Others, like the Maluku Islands located south of the Philippines, are smaller. Of all the spice-bearing islands, the Maluku Islands are probably the most famous. Indeed, for many years, Europeans referred to them as the *Spice Islands*.

The islands of the Malay Archipelago are special. They mark a boundary between two sections of Earth's crust. The ridge formed by those sections is noted for its volcanoes and earthquake activity. It is part of the Ring of Fire, an arc of volcanoes that surrounds the rim of the Pacific Ocean.

The Spice Islands

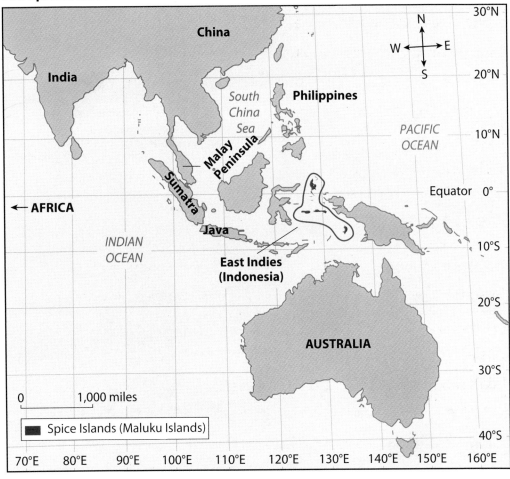

Today, the Spice Islands are part of the nation of Indonesia.

The equator runs through the Malay Archipelago, just south of the Malay Peninsula. Daytime temperatures are between 70° and 90°F year-round. Rainfall can be as much as 320 inches a year on the forested mountain slopes. On the **rain shadow** sides, it can be less than twenty inches a year. Overall, the annual average is eighty inches. Heat, heavy rainfall, and rich soil result in exceptional spice crops.

> **Vocabulary**
>
> **rain shadow,** n. an area that gets less rain because it is on the protected side of a mountain

The Quest for Spices

You might wonder why the Europeans didn't just sail over to the Spice Islands and buy their spices. It wasn't that simple. They did not yet know that the Atlantic Ocean went as far as the southern tip of Africa. Nor were their ships and **navigational** skills suited to such long voyages. And at the time, the exact location of the Spice Islands was a closely guarded secret.

During the Middle Ages, the spice trade was controlled by Arab **traders**. They controlled the market not only for nutmeg and cloves from the Spice Islands, but also for ginger from China and cinnamon from India. For hundreds of years, from around 1100 until 1400, the Arabs managed to keep the location of the Spice Islands a secret. They even made up stories about how dangerous it was to sail to these islands. If you had been alive then you might have heard tales told by Arab traders of the fantastic monsters and hideous flesh-eating birds that guarded the Spice Islands. Stories like these were designed to help the Arab traders preserve their **monopoly** of the spice trade.

> ## Vocabulary
>
> **navigational**, adj. related to controlling the movement of a ship
>
> **trader**, n. a person who buys and sells goods
>
> **monopoly**, n. a situation in which one person, country, or company has complete control of the supply of a good or service
>
> **trading center**, n. a place where people buy and sell goods

How did the spice trade work? Arab traders sailed east to **trading centers** in India, Ceylon (now Sri Lanka), and the Spice Islands. After loading up their ships, they sailed west again. A typical trip took them around the Arabian Peninsula, into the Red Sea, and north to Egypt. There they sold the spices to **merchants** from Venice and other parts of Italy. The Arab traders made huge profits from this exchange.

Traders crossed the Indian Ocean to reach the Spice Islands.

The Venetians did well, too. They **negotiated** with Arab traders to distribute spices throughout Europe. Europeans wanting to purchase spices had to deal with Venice. Once they had acquired the spices, the Venetian merchants could set whatever prices and taxes they pleased. This arrangement made Venice a very wealthy city. It also made the Venetians unpopular.

Vocabulary

merchant, n. a person who buys and sells goods to earn money

negotiate, v. to discuss the terms of an agreement

Wealthy Europeans had become used to exotic goods from the Venetian marketplace. At the same time, they resented the high cost of doing business with Venetian merchants. Similarly, the Venetian merchants dreamed of a time when they would not have to deal with the Arab traders, but instead be able to deal directly with merchants in the Spice Islands.

The Travels of Marco Polo

Maffeo and Niccolo Polo were brothers who lived in Venice in the second half of the thirteenth century. The Polos were great traders and travelers. When the overland trade routes that had existed in Roman times opened up again, they set out to find the legendary markets of the East. At the time, the **Mongols** controlled much of Asia and part of Europe. The Mongols made the roads safe for travelers, and many adventurers were anxious to seek their fortunes. Some went to trade for silk, gems, **porcelain**, and tea. Others hoped to find sources of the world's most exotic spices.

Vocabulary

Mongol, n. a native of the Asian nation of Mongolia

porcelain, n. a type of fine pottery

"diplomatic mission," (phrase) a group of people who serve as representatives of their government in another country

When the Polo brothers started their second journey east in 1271, they decided to take Niccolo's young son, Marco, with them. The expedition ended up taking them twenty-four years to complete. The three spent time in the service of the Mongol ruler Kublai Khan and traveled throughout Asia by land and by sea.

Marco's father and uncle served as military advisers to the Great Khan. Kublai Khan took a liking to Marco. He sent Marco to distant parts of his kingdom on **diplomatic missions**. Wherever he went, Marco observed, asked questions, and remembered what he had seen.

During his travels, Marco Polo served the Emperor Kublai Khan. Khan ruled a vast Mongol empire that included China.

In 1295, Marco Polo returned to Venice. Soon after, he was captured during a war with a neighboring city. Polo was sent to jail. His cellmate was a writer from the city of Pisa. During his days in prison, Polo talked about his travels, and the writer wrote down what Marco said. Together, the two cellmates produced a book that helped change the world. *The Travels of Marco Polo* was read by people all over Europe, first in handwritten copies and later in printed editions. Polo was the first European to write about China, Thailand, the Malay Archipelago, and other Asian lands. His book inspired European mapmakers to update their maps. Almost two hundred years after it was written, this book inspired an Italian sea captain named Christopher Columbus.

For centuries, the search for the Spice Islands attracted explorers, adventurers, and dreamers like a magnet. While searching for the Spice Islands, these explorers found lands, oceans, and peoples that they never knew existed. It is perhaps not an exaggeration to say that the desire to reach the Spice Islands led to the European exploration of the entire planet.

This illustration from Marco Polo's book shows the port of Venice, which held a near-monopoly on the spice trade in Europe.

Chapter 2
Motives and Means

The Value of Spices By the mid-1400s, Europeans had several **motives** for exploration. For one thing, they wanted direct access to the spice-growing areas of the world described by Marco Polo.

The Big Question

What developments enabled Europeans to travel farther?

Vocabulary

motive, n. the reason for taking a specific action

Because of the monopoly held by Arab traders and Venetian merchants, spices were very valuable throughout Europe. In some places, spices were so valuable that peppercorns were used in place of coins. Payments were even counted out peppercorn by peppercorn. Spices by the pound were used to pay fees, tariffs, taxes, rents, and ransoms.

Pepper was valuable as a spice. This painting from the 1400s shows peppercorns being grown (left) and offered to the king (right).

Europeans were so enthusiastic about spices because their food was not very tasty. At this time Europeans did not yet have any of the fruits and vegetables native to North and South America. Potatoes, tomatoes, corn, bananas, chocolate, peanuts, strawberries, blueberries, and pineapples were all unheard of. Europeans did not have sugar until the late Middle Ages. They also had no coffee or tea.

Europeans typically butchered livestock in the fall. They used salt to **cure** the meat for long-term storage. After a few months, much of this meat was not very appetizing. A pinch of pepper, cloves, or ginger could make bad tasting or even spoiled meat much easier to eat.

Vocabulary

cure, v. to preserve meat, fish, or other food by smoking, drying, or salting it

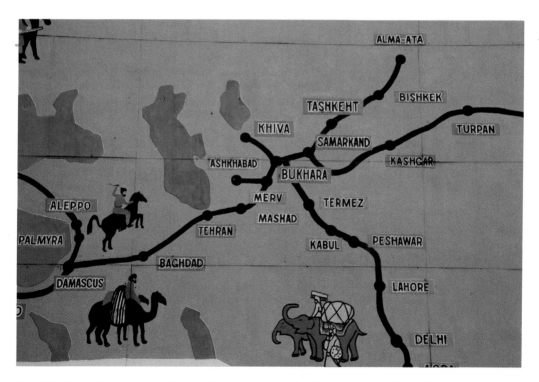

The Silk Road: For many centuries this was an overland trade route of nearly 4,000 miles that crossed mountains and deserts between Asia and the Arab and European cities near the Mediterranean Sea.

It's hardly surprising, then, that Europeans developed a taste for the intense flavors of spices that come from plants grown on tiny islands in faraway places. As you have discovered, getting those spices wasn't at all easy. Because of this, Arab traders and Venetian merchants charged very high prices. Then, in the fifteenth century, the quest for spices became even more problematic. The Turks shut down the Silk Road, an important land route, which had previously been used to transport spices from the East.

The Europeans needed a sea route to Asia. Nobody was sure that such a route existed. Everybody hoped one would be discovered. The great kings of Europe began looking for brave explorers, shipbuilders, mapmakers, and others who could help them with this quest.

The Crusades

Exploration was also fueled by another series of events. In the Middle Ages, generations of European knights and soldiers went on Crusades to the Middle East to capture the Holy Land from Muslims. When Europeans reached the Middle East, they saw that Islamic civilization was much more advanced than they had been led to believe. Crusaders returned home and described the goods and cultures they had encountered. This added to European curiosity about the world outside their borders.

New Ships

Arab traders had been sailing across the Indian Ocean for centuries. Therefore, they had learned a great deal about

navigation and shipbuilding. By comparison, Europeans generally made shorter voyages within European waters. European sailors navigated mostly by staying near the coastline and watching for known landmarks. Their navigational skills were not as advanced as their competitors'. Their ships were not well-suited to long voyages across **uncharted** waters.

Vocabulary
....

navigation, n. the act of planning and directing the movement of a ship, plane, or other vehicle

uncharted, adj. never mapped

hull, n. the sides and bottom of a boat

Generally, ships built in the Mediterranean shipyards of southern Europe had large triangular sails, called *lateen sails*. These sails provided easy handling in the winds that blew along the Mediterranean coast. Northern ships had square sails, which were more effective on the open ocean. They also had **hulls** built with thick, overlapping planks. These hulls were built to withstand the rougher waters of the Baltic Sea and the Atlantic Ocean.

Both of these ship designs had advantages, but neither was ideal for long voyages on uncharted waters. Then, in the 1400s, Portuguese shipbuilders combined features from these two

The caravel was developed for sailing on long voyages under various conditions.

different kinds of ships. By doing this, they created new, more seaworthy vessels called *caravels* (/kar*uh*velz/). Caravels had the sturdiness of the northern ships and the easy handling of the southern ships. Their masts were **rigged** with lateen sails so that the ships were easy to handle, but the caravels also had square sails to take advantage of strong winds that could send the ships across the open ocean. The ships had hulls sturdy enough to sail on rough seas. They were also large enough to carry men, supplies, and trade goods farther than ever before.

Vocabulary

rig, v. to prepare for sailing

astrolabe, n. a navigational tool used to determine the position of the sun, a star, or other object in the sky

sextant, n. a navigational instrument that uses a telescope and scale to determine latitude and longitude

Finding Their Way

Sailors needed ways to keep track of their location and direction when they were out of sight of land. To do this, they relied on the sky.

During the day, sailors could plot their direction in relation to the sun's apparent movement across the sky from east to west. For example, the sun setting on the right side of the ship would mean that the ship was heading south. The sun setting on the left would mean that the ship was heading north.

Ship pilots also had a variety of navigational tools to help keep their ships on course. Pilots used instruments such as the **astrolabe** and later the **sextant** to determine the ship's latitude. By measuring the height and varying positions of the sun, moon, and stars in the sky with these instruments, pilots were able to obtain information about the time of day and the ship's location. As you might imagine, though, taking exact measurements on a bobbing ship was difficult.

Speed was measured using a log attached to a rope. The rope had knots tied along it at regular spaces. A sailor counted the knots as they slipped through his hands. The number of knots let out during a certain amount of time was used to calculate the speed. Today, ship speed is still measured in *knots*.

The **magnetic compass**, a Chinese invention, had been in use in other parts of the world for centuries. Europeans also relied on it to determine direction.

Vocabulary

magnetic compass, n. a device that uses a magnetized pointer to show direction

Imagine sailing across an ocean, especially an unknown ocean, just using instruments such as an astrolabe, shown here.

16

However, many captains and navigators did not really understand how or why it worked.

To measure the passage of time, sailors used a sand **hourglass**. The ship's cabin boy turned the glass every half hour. The time calculated was checked against sunrise and sunset just in case the sand ran too fast or too slowly.

Vocabulary

hourglass, n. a glass device that measures time using the flow of sand

Navigators also made use of observations made by the crew. Information about the clouds, birds, waves, and anything floating in the water all helped to track a ship's position on the sea.

Europeans were building new ships, learning more about navigation, and updating their maps. Soon, they might really be able to sail to far-flung parts of the world.

Chapter 3
Portuguese Exploration

Pioneers of the Sea The most powerful European governments in the 1400s were the Spanish states of Castile and Aragon, France, England, and some of the city-states in Italy, such as Venice. But none of these countries led the search for a sea route to the East. It was Portugal—a small, relatively poor country— that became the seagoing pioneer.

The Big Question

Why do you think Portugal is described as a seagoing pioneer?

Portuguese leadership in exploration was largely due to one person. Prince Henry, often called the Navigator, had a strong desire to explore the oceans. Although Henry never went on any expeditions himself, he supported the design of ships. He encouraged developments in mapmaking, shipbuilding, and instrument making. He also encouraged the sharing of information, therefore enabling would-be explorers to benefit from these new ideas. Most importantly, he helped to convince his father, King John I, to pay for expensive expeditions in the name of Portugal. Like other Europeans, the Portuguese had a strong desire to set up trade routes, spread Christianity, and gain knowledge.

This statue of Prince Henry is part of a monument in Lisbon, the capital of Portugal. The monument honors Portugal's role in the Age of Exploration. Prince Henry is shown holding a ship and a map.

19

Prince Henry sent dozens of **expeditions** down the west coast of Africa. On these expeditions, Portugal's seafarers faced many challenges. Prior to this, no European had sailed very far from Europe. Just as the Arab traders did, European sailors told hair-raising stories about sea monsters and boiling waves. Really, they were encountering extremely rough waters and sea creatures that they had never seen before. Such tales made it difficult for Portuguese captains to find crew members willing to sail farther south. Therefore, reaching Cape Bojador (/boh*juh*dor/) off the Western Sahara on the Atlantic coast was indeed a great achievement for the Portuguese.

Vocabulary
....
expedition, n. a special journey taken by a group that has a clear purpose or goal

Portuguese sailors told stories of sea monsters they encountered on their expeditions.

Over the years, Prince Henry's explorers pushed farther south along the African coast. They brought back gold, ivory, spices, and people, to be sold into slavery. The first Africans to be sold arrived in Portugal in 1441. They became servants and laborers. Africans were also taken along on expeditions to serve as **interpreters** and help set up trade agreements in new ports. Portuguese traders set up trading posts and challenged the **Moors** for leadership in West Africa.

Vocabulary

interpreter, n. a person who translates from one language to another

Moor, n. a North African follower of Islam during the Middle Ages

fleet, n. a group of ships sailing together with the same purpose and under the control of the same leader

landfall, n. the reaching of land, after a trip by sea

Bartolomeu Dias

As expeditions made their way down the west coast of Africa, Portuguese horizons expanded. Their knowledge grew, and their maps became more complete. The more they learned, the less superstitious they became.

In 1487, Bartolomeu Dias (/bar*tuh*luh*mae*uh/dee*us/) set sail with a **fleet** of three ships. The fleet traveled far beyond where any European had ever sailed before. The ships stopped at various ports along the coast before stormy seas forced the fleet offshore. They did not see land for several days. When the seas calmed, the ships turned back to make **landfall**. They looked for the land that had been to the east of them as they journeyed southward. They could not find it. Then, when the ships turned north, land was sighted. But it was on the west side of the ship, not the east. This could only mean one thing: The fleet was traveling north up the east coast of Africa. They had sailed around the southern tip of Africa without knowing it!

Dias was both excited by this discovery and concerned about being so far from Portugal. He turned his fleet around. As the fleet rounded the southern tip of Africa and headed north for home, Dias spotted what he called *Cabo Tormentoso* (Cape of Storms). Today we call it the Cape of Good Hope. Dias had shown his countrymen that it was possible to sail around Africa. He was the first European to find a route to the Indian Ocean.

Vasco da Gama

When it came to exploration, the Portuguese always pushed forward. Knowledge gained on one expedition laid the groundwork for the next. Once Dias rounded the Cape of Good Hope, it was only a matter of time before other Portuguese extended the route.

In 1497, Vasco da Gama (/vah*skoe/duh*gah*muh/) led a fleet of four ships from Lisbon. The fleet rounded the Cape of Good Hope and headed northeast along the east coast of Africa. They stopped at the main trading centers along the way, including Mombasa, Mozambique, and Malindi.

In Mombasa and in Mozambique, the Portuguese ran into trouble with Arab traders. These merchants had controlled the trading centers along the coast of East Africa for hundreds of years. They felt the Portuguese were intruding on their established businesses. As a result, at several ports, Arab traders tried to seize the Portuguese ships.

Early Portuguese Exploration

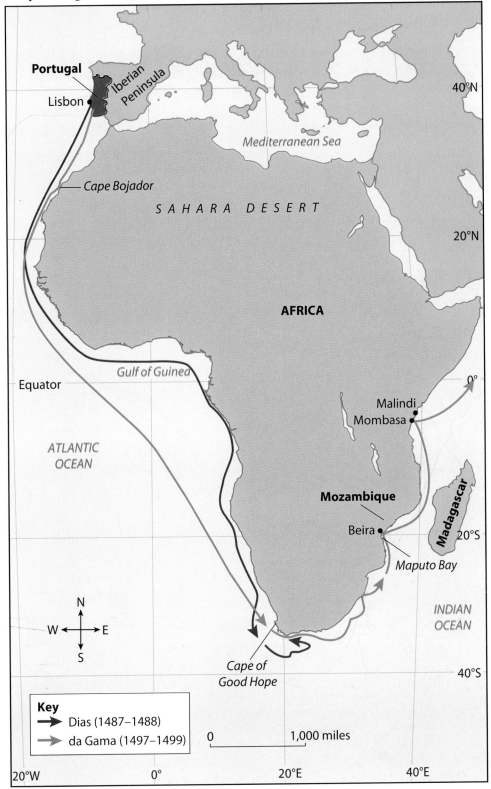

Most of what Europeans of this time knew about Africa was restricted to the coasts of the continent.

Farther north at Malindi, however, the reception was friendly. The Portuguese were given a ship's pilot to help them. The fleet crossed the Indian Ocean in twenty-three days. They made landfall at Calicut, India, known today as Kozhikode, India. The knowledge of the experienced pilot and the strong west winds known as the **trade winds** had enabled them to arrive safely.

Vocabulary

trade wind, n. a wind that almost always blows in a particular direction

scurvy, n. a disease caused by a lack of vitamin C

Calicut was a major trading city and seaport on the southwest coast of India. The main trade items were spices, gems, and pearls. Vasco da Gama was anxious to set up trade relations. The Zamorin (/zah*mor*ihn/), as the Hindu ruler was called, had other ideas. The Zamorin was not impressed with the ordinary items that da Gama had brought to exchange. He also did not want to make the Arab merchants angry. The Zamorin demanded bright red fabric, coral, silver, and gold. Only if da Gama could supply these items would they be able to do business.

The Portuguese fleet remained at Calicut for several months. When it came time to leave, the Zamorin tried to seize the Portuguese goods. Vasco da Gama and his crew managed to escape—taking with them their goods and five hostages, too.

The return trip across the Indian Ocean took three terrible months. Many of the men died of **scurvy** during their journey. They were forced to set fire to one ship because they did not have enough crew members to sail it home. The fleet finally reached Lisbon in 1499. In spite of the terrible losses on his trip, Vasco da Gama's return was cause for celebration, and he was called a hero by the king.

Vocabulary

iron ore, n. rock from which iron can be obtained

The Portuguese in East Africa

After Vasco da Gama's voyage to India, the Portuguese launched a number of follow-up expeditions. Their aim was to seize control of the trade that flourished on the eastern coast of Africa.

The African economy in general depended on farming and raising livestock. Still, trade was well-established by the time the Portuguese arrived. Demand was high for African copper, **iron ore**, gold, ivory, salt, tools, and pottery. These goods and others were traded between the continent's inland and coastal trade centers. From Africa, goods were transported north to Egyptian and Mediterranean trade centers. Others were transported east to trade centers in India. The slave trade also grew along these routes.

Vasco da Gama was another of the daring Portuguese sea captains who sailed into unknown waters.

Historians sometimes call the East African coast the Swahili (/swah*hee*lee/) Coast, because the African language Swahili was spoken by many of the people in this area. The population of the Swahili Coast was a mixture of Africans, Arabs, and Persians. Most people in the region were Muslim.

The Portuguese set up trading posts along the Swahili Coast in places like Beira and Maputo Bay. Today, both are found in the country of Mozambique. Beira was an especially valuable trade center. Gold that was mined inland was shipped down the Save River to Beira. From there it was shipped to Portugal.

Once the Portuguese were established along the Swahili Coast, they were anxious to learn more about the inland areas. For decades, the Portuguese tried to gain control of the rich resources of the interior of Africa. However, despite their efforts, they were

Portugal's Trade Empire

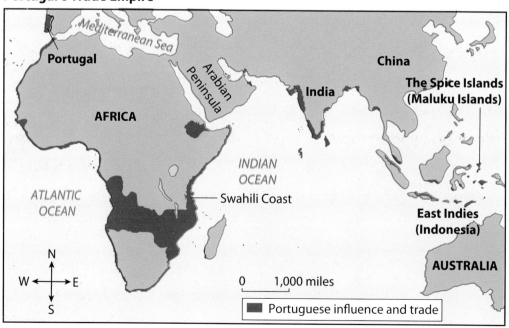

Portugal set up a trade network that stretched from Africa across the Indian Ocean to India and the Spice Islands.

met with strong resistance. Portugal was never able to gain full control of the African interior and their expansion was limited to a number of small colonies.

The Portuguese did manage to break the long-standing Arab traders' monopoly along the coast. They set up a network of trading posts, not only along the Swahili Coast but also in India, the East Indies, and the Spice Islands.

Pedro Alvares Cabral and Brazil

A fleet of thirteen ships set sail from Portugal in March 1500, bound for India under the command of Pedro Alvares Cabral (/kuh*brahl/). Cabral was supposed to follow the route taken by Vasco da Gama. His goal was to make contact with trade centers in the East and to see what else he could find. Before leaving Lisbon, Cabral met with da Gama, who shared maps and information about sailing to India.

Cabral sailed out of Lisbon harbor and turned south. He followed the coast of Africa until he had passed the Cape Verde Islands (off present-day Senegal). Da Gama had told Cabral not to get stuck in the Gulf of Guinea. The ocean there was frequently calm, with little or no wind to move a ship. He told Cabral to head southwest and sail out into the Atlantic Ocean instead. Cabral did so, and in April 1500, he sighted land. The expedition had reached the coast of Brazil.

We tend to think of the western and eastern hemispheres as being very far apart. However, Brazil juts out into the Atlantic Ocean toward the western coast of Africa. All it took was a southwestward

Cabral's Expedition

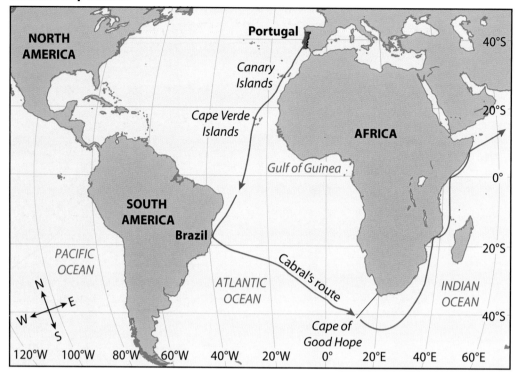

The distance between the east coast of Brazil and the west coast of Africa is not that great.

swing by Cabral and some strong winds to close the distance. The Portuguese explorer came upon land he did not know existed. He immediately claimed the territory for his king.

Cabral sent a ship home to tell the king of this land, which he named *Vera Cruz* (/vair*uh/krooz/), the Island of the True Cross. He made contact with the people living in the area and stayed for ten days. Then he set out to complete his expedition. Four ships were lost as the fleet approached the Cape of Good Hope. Among the men who drowned was Bartolomeu Dias, the explorer who had been the first European to spot the cape twelve years earlier.

Cabral continued on with what remained of his fleet. He traded at a number of ports along the Indian Ocean and loaded his ships with precious spices. On the return journey, more ships were lost. Only four ships sailed back into Lisbon harbor.

For a time, this land now called the Island of the True Cross was spared the impact of European settlement. The Portuguese were busy gaining power in the rich ports of Africa, India, the East Indies, and the Spice Islands. They did not want to bother with this new territory—at least not yet.

Chapter 4
Christopher Columbus

Sailing West to the East Indies

On August 3, 1492, three ships left Palos, Spain, and headed for the Canary Islands, off the African coast. In those days, European ships often sailed to the Canary Islands to trade or rest before continuing south along the coast of Africa.

The Big Question
....
Why do you think Columbus kept a secret log?

These three ships did something different. After their stop in the Canary Islands, they sailed due west.

The ships were under the command of an Italian named Christopher Columbus. Columbus had read Marco Polo's account of the East Indies and was eager to find the sources of the spices Polo had described. His approach was a new one, however. He believed that it was unnecessary to sail all the way around Africa, as Dias had done. Like most educated people of his day, Columbus knew that the world was round. He believed he could reach the East by sailing west. He also believed that the world was smaller than people imagined. Therefore he thought that the East Indies could not be very far west of the Canary Islands.

Columbus searched for many years for support of his plan to find a new route to Asia.

Columbus had spent seven years trying to convince the rulers of Europe to sponsor, or pay for, a westward expedition to the Indies. The king of Portugal told him no. The king of France kept putting him off. At first, King Ferdinand and Queen Isabella of Spain declined as well. However, in 1492, they agreed to pay for an expedition. They instructed Columbus to claim any new lands he discovered for Spain.

Columbus was given three ships, the *Niña*, the *Pinta*, and the *Santa Maria*. That September, they left the Canary Islands and headed west into waters quite unfamiliar to Europeans. According to some who sailed with Columbus, many sailors wept. They were fearful

The captains and crews of the three ships led by Columbus faced a hazardous voyage into unknown waters.

of what lay ahead. Columbus comforted them with promises of riches. He also found another way to calm his sailors. On the first day of the voyage, he calculated how far they had sailed. He told his crew that they had covered fifteen **leagues**, even though they had really traveled eighteen leagues. He did not want them to become afraid over time of how far they were sailing. So he lied, while keeping the truth in a secret **log**.

Vocabulary

league, n. a unit of distance equal to approximately three miles

log, n. a written record of a ship's progress

Columbus kept this up for weeks. If the ships traveled twenty-five leagues, he would tell his crew twenty. If they covered thirty-nine, he would say thirty. It was a clever strategy.

But by early October the sailors had begun to get worried, in spite of the inaccurate distances Columbus was giving them. They had been sailing west for a month, without any sign of land. Many of the men feared they had traveled so far west that they would never find their way back to Europe. Some of the more superstitious sailors doubted the world was round. They feared the ships might sail off Earth's edge.

Columbus's crew grew restless. Fearing they would never reach land, they threatened to overthrow their leader.

33

The sailors talked among themselves. Why did Columbus insist on sailing west? Hadn't Dias found the true way to the Indies by sailing around Africa? How much longer would their supplies last? Did they have enough food and fresh water for the trip back to Spain?

Eventually the sailors threatened a **mutiny**. They warned Columbus that if he did not turn back, they would throw him overboard and tell the authorities in Spain that he had fallen in by accident.

Vocabulary
....

mutiny, n. the rebellion of a ship's crew against the captain

Columbus avoided a mutiny by promising to turn slightly south. He also promised to turn back if they did not see land soon.

When Columbus's fleet made landfall, he thought he had succeeded in sailing west to the East Indies.

This was a risky promise to make, but it paid off. A few days later, sailors began to see encouraging signs. They spotted birds that were known to live on land. They saw a bush floating in the ocean, with berries still clinging to the branches.

Finally, in the early morning hours of October 12, 1492, an excited shout rippled across the water. *"Tierra! Tierra!"* called the Spanish lookout on the *Pinta*. "Land! Land!"

The First Encounter

When the sun rose on that day, Columbus took a landing party ashore to meet the inhabitants of what he thought was Asia. He was actually in the Bahamas, a group of islands just east of what is now Florida. Columbus decided to name the island he was on *San Salvador* (Holy Savior). He personally carried the **royal standard** ashore to claim the land for Spain.

> **Vocabulary**
>
> **royal standard,** n. a flag that represents a king or queen

The lush green land did not look much like the Asia described by Marco Polo. There were no silks or spices to be seen. Columbus nevertheless was convinced that he had reached the East Indies. He called the native people *Indians*. The name stuck, even after later explorers proved that Columbus had not found the East Indies but rather islands near two new continents located between Europe and Asia.

The inhabitants of the island were not "Indians," but members of the Taino (/tye*noh/) tribe. They were peaceful people who fished in the waters around their island.

The Tainos came down to the shore to look at Columbus and his men. Columbus had brought along a translator who spoke Hebrew and Arabic. He felt sure that the "Indians" would understand one of these two Eastern languages. To his frustration, they did not. The Spanish and the Tainos ended up using sign language to communicate.

In order to locate what he believed would be China, Columbus soon sailed on. He took six Tainos with him. Before long he landed on what are now the islands of Cuba and Hispaniola. Today the island of Hispaniola is divided between the countries of Haiti and the Dominican Republic.

By January 1493, supplies were getting low. Columbus set sail for Spain. Columbus traveled until he reached the latitude of 40°N. Then he turned the ships east, putting them on course for Spain.

The Triumphant Return

When Columbus returned to the court of King Ferdinand and Queen Isabella, he told them everything he had seen in the lands that he had claimed for their country. He described his meetings with an Indian chieftain, whom he called the "great khan." He told of his visit to Cuba, which he thought was Japan. He described the contacts he had made.

King Ferdinand and Queen Isabella rewarded Columbus by giving him money and land. They also named him "Admiral of the Ocean Sea. "

The Spanish monarchs Ferdinand and Isabella were pleased with Columbus's account of his voyage.

News of Columbus's success quickly spread across Europe. However, not everyone was convinced that Columbus had found a westward route to Asia. Among the biggest doubters were the Portuguese. They thought that Columbus had explored part of the African coast or an unknown group of islands in the Atlantic. The Spanish themselves did not really know what to think. They eventually came to believe that Columbus had found some faraway place. Many also decided that whatever place that was, they wanted to go there too.

The Treaty of Tordesillas

It was inevitable that Spain and Portugal would become trading rivals. Various disputes broke out between the two countries. The pope tried but failed to settle the disagreements. Finally, **diplomats** from the two countries worked out an agreement. In 1494, they drew an imaginary line from the North Pole to the South Pole, 370 leagues (1,185 miles or 1,907 kilometers) west of the Cape Verde Islands. The Treaty of Tordesillas (/tor*dae*seel*yus/) said that all land to the west of this line could be claimed by Spain. All land to the east could be claimed by Portugal. Neither country could occupy any territory already in the hands of a Christian ruler. The agreement disregarded the **indigenous** peoples of the Americas, who had maintained sophisticated cultures for hundreds, if not thousands, of years.

> **Vocabulary**
>
> **diplomat,** n. someone who represents the government of one country in another country
>
> **indigenous,** adj. native to a particular region or environment

The treaty placed all of North and South America west of the treaty line under Spanish control. What is modern day Brazil was given to the Portuguese. In terms of landmass, Spain had the advantage. Over the next hundred years or so, millions of people in North and South America would learn to speak Spanish, while the Brazilians learned Portuguese.

However, in 1494, when the treaty was signed, nobody was quite sure yet what had been divided or who had rights to what. Cabral had not yet discovered Brazil (that would happen in 1500), and no one yet knew exactly what Columbus had discovered in 1492.

The Treaty of Tordesillas divided newly explored territories between Spain and Portugal.

Queen Isabella of Spain sent a letter to Columbus, urging him to determine where the treaty line was and which lands lay on the Spanish side.

The Later Voyages of Columbus

Columbus made three more voyages to the Americas. On his second voyage, he mapped most of the islands of the Caribbean Sea and established the permanent colony of Santo Domingo on Hispaniola. He left his brothers Bartholomew and Diego in charge while he searched the Caribbean Sea for gold. His search was unsuccessful.

The third voyage (1498–1500) was even worse. While Columbus explored the north coast of South America, Bartholomew and

Diego angered both the indigenous peoples and the Spanish settlers of Hispaniola. The Columbus brothers forced the indigenous people to work in gold mines, and favored some Spanish settlers over others. Eventually complaints reached the Spanish court. Columbus lost his position as governor of the colony, and his brothers were sent back to Spain.

The fourth voyage (1502–1504) was the worst of all. Columbus and his men were shipwrecked on the island of Jamaica for a year. By the time Columbus returned to Spain, he was in bad health, and his reputation had been damaged. When Columbus died in 1506, almost nobody noticed. In 1537 his bones were sent back to Hispaniola and buried in the Cathedral of Santo Domingo.

Columbus's Voyages

None of Columbus's later voyages were as successful as his first.

The Final Blow

The Americas were actually named after another explorer, Amerigo Vespucci (/ves*poo*chee/). Vespucci had explored the coast of South America for Portugal in 1501. He wrote letters about his voyage that were published. In his letters he described a densely populated continent. He also used the term "New World" to describe this place. A German mapmaker was so impressed with Amerigo's revelations he labeled the new continent *America* on the map he was working on.

Chapter 5
A Spanish Empire and Its Critics

After Columbus The Spanish continued to expand their lands in the Americas after Columbus died. As the Spanish grew stronger, the situation of the indigenous peoples grew worse. Many of the Spaniards were ruthless colonists.

The Big Question

How did European explorers and colonists treat the indigenous people of the Americas?

Vocabulary

immunity, n. a body's ability to remain free of illness even after being exposed to the cause of the illness

Indigenous people died in large numbers in gold mines controlled by the Spanish. Thousands more died from European diseases against which they had no **immunities**. The effects were devastating. When the Spanish first arrived in Hispaniola, it had hundreds of thousands of inhabitants. By 1507, the indigenous population had decreased to sixty thousand. By 1531, there were only about six hundred native inhabitants left on the island.

Indigenous peoples were treated harshly and unfairly by Spanish colonists.

43

When the gold mines became less profitable, the Spanish introduced cattle ranches and sugar **plantations**. Sugar was a **cash crop**. This meant that the plantation owners could earn a lot of money growing and selling sugar. But the rapid decline of the indigenous population created a labor shortage. By the sixteenth century, that shortage was being filled by the importation of enslaved people from Africa.

The Conquistadors

Between 1495 and 1535, Spanish **conquistadors** (/kon*kees*tuh*dorz/) gained control of much of South and Central America. You have learned about Hernán Cortés, the conquistador who destroyed the mighty Aztec Empire in modern-day Mexico. You have also learned about Francisco Pizarro, who invaded the Inca civilization in Peru.

> ### Vocabulary
>
> **plantation,** n. a large farm where one or more crops were grown by a large number of laborers; these crops were sold for a profit by the plantation owner
>
> **cash crop,** n. a crop that is grown to be sold
>
> **conquistador,** n. the Spanish word for conqueror
>
> **isthmus,** n. a narrow piece of land that connects two larger land masses

Pizarro spent many years working for another famous conquistador, Vasco Nùñez de Balboa (/vah*skoe/noo*nyath/de/bal*boe*uh/). Balboa and Pizarro explored the **Isthmus** of Panama together. During their explorations, they learned about a great sea to the west. In 1513, Balboa organized an expedition to find this sea. He chose one hundred ninety of his toughest men, including Pizarro, as well as men to carry equipment and supplies. The party crossed swamps by stripping off their clothing and carrying it on their

Balboa and Pizarro made a difficult journey across the Isthmus of Panama looking for a great sea.

heads as they splashed along. They fought off snakes, crocodiles, and mosquitoes. They hacked their way through thick jungles. They climbed over mountains.

Balboa and his men were rewarded for their struggles. On September 25, 1513, they stood atop a mountain and looked out over a body of water Balboa called "the South Sea." Today, we call it the Pacific Ocean. Balboa marched down to the ocean and tasted the salt water, just to be sure. Then, as Europeans so often did, he claimed all the lands washed by this sea in the name of his homeland, Spain.

Encomiendas

Of course, building an **empire** in the Americas required settlers. To encourage migration to these new lands, the Spanish set up a system of *encomiendas*

Vocabulary

empire, n. a group of countries or territories under the control of one government or ruler

(/en*koe*me*yen*dus). This system meant that a Spanish settler was given a large plot of land and a number of enslaved workers. *Encomiendas* clearly benefited Spain and the Spanish settlers. They also led to the further enslavement of indigenous peoples.

Bartolomé de Las Casas

Clearly many Spaniards became rich by conquering or enslaving the indigenous people of the Americas. However, some people spoke out against such cruelty. One such person was Bartolomé de Las Casas (/bahr*toe*loe*mae/de/lahs/kah*sahs/).

Las Casas came from a family of explorers. His father and his uncle sailed with Christopher Columbus. In 1502, Las Casas sailed for the Americas himself. He settled in Hispaniola, where he became a priest and where he was granted a large *encomienda*, complete with enslaved workers. Eventually, though, Las Casas

Bartolomé de Las Casas argued for better treatment of indigenous peoples.

came to the conclusion that the *encomienda* system was wrong. He began to preach against the enslavement of people.

Las Casas returned to Spain to seek the support of the king. He also wrote a book telling people in Spain what was happening in the Americas. Las Casas's *The Devastation of the Indies: A Brief Account* helped turn the king against the *encomienda* system. In the book, Las Casas explained that greed was the cause of such exploitation.

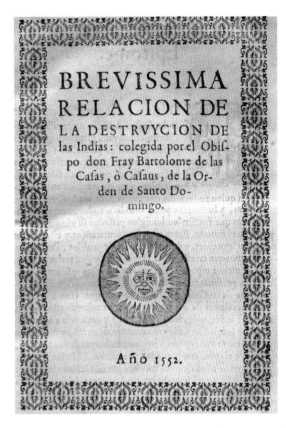

Much of what we know today about the effect of the Spanish conquest on the indigenous peoples of the Americas comes from Bartolomé de Las Casas's book.

Eventually the king changed the laws regarding the treatment of indigenous peoples. But it was difficult to enforce these laws from across the ocean. The indigenous peoples continued to suffer. Las Casas later wrote a history of the Spanish conquest of the Americas. His work is the source for much of what we know of conquered peoples such as the Aztec in Mexico and Inca in Peru. Today Bartolomé de Las Casas is widely admired for his stand against the **exploitation** of the indigenous people of the Americas.

> **Vocabulary**
>
> **exploitation,** n. the practice of taking unfair advantage of a person or group

Chapter 6
Magellan's Voyage

Ferdinand Magellan While conquistadors conquered new lands for Spain, sea captains continued to explore the oceans. One of the most famous of these captains was Ferdinand Magellan.

The Big Question

How important was it for explorers to have finally circumnavigated the globe?

Magellan was born in Portugal during the great age of Portuguese exploration. As a boy, he served as a page in the Portuguese court. He dreamed of life at sea. Magellan was thirteen when Columbus sailed back to Spain with tales of his westward travels. Inspired by Columbus, Magellan went to sea.

Magellan was a hot-tempered fellow, and he was usually in one kind of trouble or another. His first expeditions took him to trading centers in the East, first as a crew member and later as a fleet commander in the Portuguese navy. But Magellan's temper eventually cost him the support of the Portuguese crown. The time came when the king refused to send him on any more expeditions.

In 1517, John of Lisbon, a friend of Magellan's, persuaded him to ask Spain for support. A famous navigator, John of Lisbon had just

Portuguese sea captain Ferdinand Magellan was inspired by the voyages of Christopher Columbus.

returned from a Portuguese expedition to explore the coastline of Brazil. He said he had come upon a **strait**. He thought this new information might lead to the discovery of a water route through the middle of the South American continent.

Vocabulary

strait, n. a narrow body of water that connects two larger bodies of water

If there was such a route, this would make trade and the accumulation of wealth easier for the European explorers, traders, and merchants, and of course for the kings of Europe. John of Lisbon fired up Magellan's imagination. When another friend helped him gain command of a Spanish expedition to explore this strait, Magellan turned his back on Portugal forever.

In September 1519, five ships carrying 277 men left port for the three-month voyage to Brazil. Right away, the boats started leaking. A week into the voyage, Magellan faced a mutiny. But he held onto his command. In January 1520, the ships reached the waters that John of Lisbon had described.

Magellan was soon disappointed. The crew sent to explore the strait returned with news that the strait did not provide a route through the continent to the Pacific Ocean. Instead it flowed into a bay.

Frustrated by the lack of progress in their search for a strait, Magellan's crew mutinied.

50

Magellan met with his officers to discuss their next steps. Some wanted to sail to Africa and on to the Spice Islands, following known routes. Others wanted to go back up the coast for the winter. Magellan decided to keep sailing south.

High winds and rough seas slowed and battered the fleet. In March, heavy snow finally stopped progress altogether. Magellan led his angry crew into a harbor on the coast of what is now Argentina. There in early April, Magellan faced his second mutiny. Once again, he was able to regain control of the crew.

Finding the Strait

Magellan resumed his search in October. He lost one ship in rough seas. Near the southern tip of South America, a storm blew his remaining ships into a narrow strait. This strait turned out to be the strait Magellan had been seeking all along. Unfortunately, it was very difficult to navigate. Tall cliffs loomed up on both sides, and violent tides threatened to smash the ships against the rocks.

Many of Magellan's men felt that discovering the strait was enough. They were afraid to sail through the strait. They urged Magellan to turn back. Magellan refused. The crew of one ship mutinied and did turn back. The other three ships pressed on. It took more than a month for the fleet to pass through what would eventually be called the Straits of Magellan.

Finally, the fleet emerged into a vast and calm ocean. Magellan and his crew knelt down and recited a prayer of thanksgiving. Magellan also pointed out to his crew that they were now sailing upon unknown waters. Because the waters were so pleasantly peaceful, he named the body of water the Pacific Ocean.

Magellan's fleet turned north. The ships followed the west coast of South America until they could pick up the currents that would carry them west, across the ocean. Magellan did not know the size of the Pacific Ocean. He figured his ships would reach Asia in a matter of days. The ships made landfall at some of the Pacific Islands, but the ocean was so large that supplies ran out quickly.

Finally, on March 16, Magellan and his crew spotted the easternmost island of the Philippine archipelago. The men who had survived the ordeal were able to gather their strength.

It was now a year and a half since they had left Spain. The men were anxious to head for the Spice Islands and then make their way

In 1520, Magellan and his crew discovered the South American strait that connected the Atlantic and Pacific Oceans.

home. Magellan, however, wanted to explore the Philippine Islands. This decision proved to be Magellan's final command to his weary men. Magellan was killed in a confrontation with island chieftains.

The crew sailed homeward under the command of Juan Sebastián del Cano. They finally reached Spain in September 1522, nearly three years after they had begun the journey. Only one ship of the original five remained. Only eighteen of the original crew of 277 survived. But this ship and these men had achieved a feat previously unheard of: they had **circumnavigated** the globe. Amazingly, the one surviving ship carried home enough exotic spices to pay for the entire expedition.

Vocabulary

circumnavigate, v. to travel completely around something (such as Earth), especially by water

The survivors of Magellan's expedition became the first to circumnavigate the globe.

Chapter 7
England Explores and Colonizes

John Cabot In 1490, Giovanni Caboto (/joh*vah*nee/kah*boh* toh/) moved his family from Venice to Spain. Years of experience as a Venetian spice trader had made Caboto an expert seaman. Now he was caught up in the spirit of exploration.

> **The Big Question**
>
> How did European exploration of the Americas lead to settlement and colonization?

Caboto wanted to form an expedition to search for a northwesterly route to the Spice Islands. Unfortunately, the monarchs of both Portugal and Spain had other plans.

The Portuguese had established their own route to the East around the Cape of Good Hope at the southern tip of Africa. When Christopher Columbus returned from his voyage, the Spanish believed that they had found another route. No one wanted to hear Caboto's proposal for still another route.

Caboto moved with his family to the port city of Bristol, England. There, Giovanni Caboto changed his name to John Cabot. The English

John Cabot sought support for an expedition to find a passage to the Spice Islands through North America.

monarch, Henry VII, and the merchants of Bristol were happy to give the explorer their support. They hoped he would bring them great wealth.

After a failed first attempt in 1496, John Cabot set sail again in 1497. He sailed under an English flag with only one ship and a crew of eighteen. The ship crossed the North Atlantic. After five weeks of travel, the crew spotted what they called "new found land." You may have learned about this area when you studied the Vikings and the colony they called *Vineland*. Cabot believed that he had found an island off the coast of Asia. He returned to England to report his findings.

The sailors did not have any spices or silks to show for their journey, but they were able to describe scooping fish out of the

Cabot's crew described waters so rich in fish they could be scooped out in baskets.

water in baskets. The voyage was judged a success, and another trip was planned for the following year.

The next time Cabot set sail, he had a fleet of five ships. One of his ships returned to Bristol after a storm. Cabot and the other four ships were never seen again. To this day, nobody knows for certain what happened to them.

The Northwest Passage

John Cabot was one of the first explorers to seek the **Northwest Passage** to the Indies. He was not the last. Cabot's son Sebastian followed in his father's footsteps, as did many other explorers. For many years, all of these explorers were frustrated in their attempts. Those who went south found a continuous band of land blocking their way—the eastern coast of North America. Explorers who went farther north were literally stopped cold, their passage prevented by ice in the water. The farther north explorers went, the fewer goods they could find to bring back home. Northern explorers generally had almost nothing to show for their efforts.

> **Vocabulary**
>
> **Northwest Passage,** n. a sea route connecting the Atlantic Ocean and Pacific Ocean along the northern coast of North America
>
> **colonization,** n. the practice of bringing people from a different country to control and settle an area that already has an indigenous population

Even though the explorers failed to find a northwesterly shortcut to the Indies, their attempts did have some helpful results. Explorers looking for the passage made maps of the coast of North America and thus set the stage for the **colonization** of the continent.

Sir Francis Drake

Once the Age of Exploration was underway, the seas were crowded with European ships carrying valuable materials. Adventurous men could make a lot of money as pirates. Indeed, one of the greatest English explorers made his name as a pirate, robbing the Spanish and Portuguese ships and presenting that treasure to Queen Elizabeth. His name was Francis Drake, and he became one of the greatest sea captains in history.

During his early years on the ocean, Drake's ship was attacked and robbed by a Spanish ship. Drake never forgot these attacks. He spent much of his adult life seeking revenge on the Spaniards. As Drake crisscrossed the Atlantic, he took every opportunity to **loot** Spanish trade ships

Vocabulary

loot, v. to steal or take something by force

Sir Francis Drake used his pirate skills to serve Queen Elizabeth I of England.

loaded with spices and silver. He also led raids on Spanish ports in the Americas.

In 1577, Drake convinced a group of people to invest in one of his voyages. He set out with a fleet of five ships with 164 crewmen. At first, the voyage seemed to be nothing more than one of Drake's usual raiding parties. Instead, Drake followed Magellan's example by embarking on a journey around the world. Drake surprised his crew by plundering a Portuguese ship and taking not only several sacks of silver but also an experienced Portuguese pilot. This hostage guided Drake's fleet on the journey across the Atlantic.

Drake's fleet crossed from the Atlantic Ocean to the Pacific Ocean through the Straits of Magellan. Drake observed the southerly area that Magellan had called *Tierra del Fuego*, or "land of fire." Magellan named it for the campfires burning in native villages along the shore. Drake noted that this area was an archipelago rather than a part of the continent. This observation would lead future navigators to the open sea around Cape Horn at the southern tip of South America.

By the time the expedition reached the west coast of South America, Drake had only fifty-eight men and one ship left. That ship was the *Golden Hind*. As the *Golden Hind* moved up the coast of what are now Chile and Peru, Drake captured ships and raided ports.

In Peru, Drake sailed into a harbor crowded with Spanish ships and proceeded to rob each ship of its treasure. He learned that a ship loaded with gold and silver had just left port a few days earlier. The ship also had many powerful guns.

Drake and his *Golden Hind* raced up the coast after the heavy and slow-moving Spanish treasure ship. When he saw it, he hung water barrels off the back of his ship to make *Golden Hind* look like a merchant ship. When he got close, he cut loose the barrels and pulled up next to the Spanish ship. Drake's trained sailors jumped aboard the treasure ship and cut down the Spanish crew, throwing many of them overboard. They then looted the ship of its treasure and set it on fire.

Sir Francis Drake's *Golden Hind* laid a trap for a Spanish treasure ship.

The Spanish Armada

Not surprisingly, Spain was very angry about Sir Francis Drake's actions. Drake might have been a hero in England, but to the Spanish he was nothing but a pirate. The Spanish ambassador is said to have called him "the master-thief of the unknown world." The Spaniards demanded that Queen Elizabeth return the stolen treasure and have Drake hanged. The queen refused.

Spain considered itself the strongest naval power in the world. Its rulers resented the attacks by English pirates and England's involvement in other Spanish affairs. It put together an **armada** of ships loaded with heavy cannons and soldiers. In 1588, the armada set sail to invade England and overthrow Queen Elizabeth.

> **Vocabulary**
>
> **armada,** n. a large fleet of ships

The English knew that they could not fight the huge Spanish fleet as a unit. So Drake and other English sea captains used imaginative battle tactics. They set small ships on fire and sent them into the Spanish battle formations. The Spanish, afraid that the small ships were loaded with gunpowder, broke formation. The English had smaller, more mobile ships. They used these ships to gang up on the lumbering Spanish battleships, sinking many. As the Spanish ships retreated, a storm sank still more of the armada. In the end,

In 1588, the English defeated the mighty Spanish Armada, shifting the balance of naval power from Spain to England.

only about half of the armada's more than 130 ships returned safely to Spain.

England had won a great victory. The defeat of the Spanish Armada also marked a change in the balance of sea power. The 1500s had belonged to Spain. Over the next two centuries, English ships would come to rule the seas.

Building Colonies

In the 1500s, Spain conquered Mexico and Central and South America. The Spanish accumulated a great fortune in gold and silver from their American colonies. Indeed, the main purpose of many Spanish colonies was to find gold and silver and send these precious metals back to Spain.

The English were also interested in acquiring wealth, but preferred to do so by setting up permanent settlements. They wanted colonies where people would farm, fish, cut timber, and harvest the other resources of the region.

Building colonial settlements was expensive. The English kings and queens did not want to spend the money. Instead, they gave grants of land to well-to-do people or businesses, called **joint-stock companies**, to build the colonies.

Vocabulary

joint-stock company, n. a company that raises money by selling shares, or interest in the company, in the form of stock

In 1585, Sir Walter Raleigh established the first English colony in North America. Raleigh sent a group of men to Roanoke Island, off the coast of modern-day North Carolina. Unfortunately, Raleigh's colonists grew discouraged and they returned to England.

In 1587, Raleigh sent a second group to the island. This time, women and children traveled with the men. He hoped that a community of families would stay there.

The colony got off to a good start. A baby girl, Virginia Dare, was the first English child born in the land that would become the United States. But in 1590, a supply ship reached the colony and found that everyone had disappeared without a trace. All that was left was one word carved on a tree. The colony that Raleigh founded is remembered as the "Lost Colony."

The settlers in the first English colony in North America disappeared without a trace.

In 1607, a joint-stock company called the London Company started a colony at Jamestown, Virginia. Jamestown was the first permanent English settlement in North America. At first, the colony struggled. Then the Powhatan Confederacy, Native Americans indigenous to the area, came to the colony's rescue. The Confederacy was made up of about thirty Native American groups that shared the same language, called Algonquian. It was named for the chief who governed it. Members of the Powhatan Confederacy taught the colonists how to grow tobacco, a crop that was native to North America and unknown in Europe. Growing tobacco was a big success. Tobacco quickly became a cash crop for the colonists.

Then in 1620, the Pilgrims settled at Plymouth. These colonists wanted religious freedom. Ten years later, the Puritans formed the Massachusetts Bay Company and settled in Boston.

During the 1600s, the English settled on land along most of the Atlantic coast. This land belonged to various Native American groups, who were often forced to find new places to live. The English also built colonies on islands in the West Indies in the Caribbean Sea.

These English colonies survived and prospered. By 1700, English colonies stretched from the **fisheries** of Newfoundland to the sugar plantations of the Caribbean.

> **Vocabulary**
>
> **fishery,** n. an area of water where fish or other sea creatures are raised and caught

These colonies were built on strong trade connections. They became home to people who were looking for wealth, religious freedom, and unlimited opportunities for themselves and their children.

Pursuing the Spice Trade

England successfully built colonies in North America, but it did not forget about the rest of the world. It also competed for a share of the spice trade in Asia.

England's East India Company decided that traveling all the way to the Spice Islands from England was too dangerous and too expensive. The company directors chose to base their operations in India. Before long, the East India Company had settlements in the Indian cities of Surat, Madras, Bombay, and Calcutta. The Company was also given the authority to raise an army. It was only a matter of time before the English expanded their holdings in India and started permanent trading posts there.

Chapter 8
France and the Fur Trade

France Joins In In the early 1500s, Spain was mining gold and silver in Mexico and Peru. Portugal ruled the spice trade in the Indian Ocean. England had sent John Cabot to look for the Northwest Passage. The king of France, Francis I, did not want to be left behind.

The Big Question

The French and the English had different approaches to settlement in North America. In what ways were they different?

In 1524, the king hired an Italian explorer named Giovanni da Verrazano (/joh*vah*nee /da/ver*rah*zah*noe/) to explore North America and look for the Northwest Passage.

Vocabulary

cartographer, n. a mapmaker

Verrazano's brother, a **cartographer**, sailed with him. North America was new to the Europeans and had not been mapped. One of the goals of Verrazano's expedition was to create accurate maps of the Atlantic coast.

New York's Verrazano Bridge honors explorer Giovanni da Verrazano, who explored the Atlantic coast for France.

Verrazano was the first European to sail up the Atlantic coast of the present-day United States, from North Carolina to Newfoundland. When he sailed into New York Bay, he noted that it was a deep-water harbor. Today the entrance to New York Harbor is spanned by the Verrazano-Narrows Bridge, named in his honor. Verrazano did not make it back to Europe. He was killed on an island in the Caribbean. The French king was sad to learn about his fate, but he was determined that France benefit from the riches found in the Americas. The king was also determined to find the Northwest Passage. But who could help him to achieve this goal?

Jacques Cartier

In 1534 France's king asked Jacques Cartier, a French sea captain, to explore the coast of North America. Cartier sailed to Newfoundland, where he encountered English and Spanish fishing fleets. This area of water off the coast of Newfoundland was a rich fishing ground.

Cartier continued his voyage, exploring the coast of Labrador and the Gulf of St. Lawrence. At the time, Cartier did not realize that the Gulf of St. Lawrence was in fact the mouth of a mighty river. Instead of exploring further, he claimed the land around the gulf for France and returned to Europe.

One year later, Cartier returned to North America. This time he sailed up the St. Lawrence River. In his log, Cartier recorded his thoughts on the land he saw, describing the tree-covered territory as beautiful.

Cartographers were important participants in the voyages of early explorers.

Cartier visited a Native American village on an island in the St. Lawrence. He climbed a hill and named it Mount Royal. This site eventually became part of the Canadian city of Montreal.

During the winter, Cartier's men became sick with scurvy. The snow was four-feet deep. Many of Cartier's men died from the cold and sickness. Cartier gave up hope of ever returning to France.

The friendship between Cartier and the Native Americans saved him and his men. The Native Americans taught the French how to brew a drink made from evergreen trees. (Today we know that such a brew is rich in vitamin C.) It cured the French explorers of their scurvy. In the spring, Cartier and his men returned to France.

Cartier returned on a third voyage to what is now Canada. The French king wanted a colony in North America. But French people could not be easily persuaded to become settlers in this cold, distant land. Instead, the king released prisoners from jail and sent them to settle in North America.

That colony was doomed from the start. The prisoners were happy to get out of jail but not eager to work in such difficult conditions. Supply ships were late in arriving. Jacques Cartier was forced to give up and return to France.

Over the next sixty years, France was racked by political troubles and wars. Little attention was paid to the land Cartier claimed for France.

Champlain and New France

During the 1500s, French ships did venture to the waters off Newfoundland to fish. As a result, trade relationships slowly developed between the French fishermen and the local Native Americans. The Native Americans were eager to have tools and other metal goods. The French wanted to trade furs, particularly beaver skins, which were in great demand in Europe for making men's hats.

The development of a fur trade in North America led to a renewed effort by the French to establish colonies in the land they called New France. The key figure in the settlement of New France was an explorer named Samuel de Champlain.

Champlain's Explorations

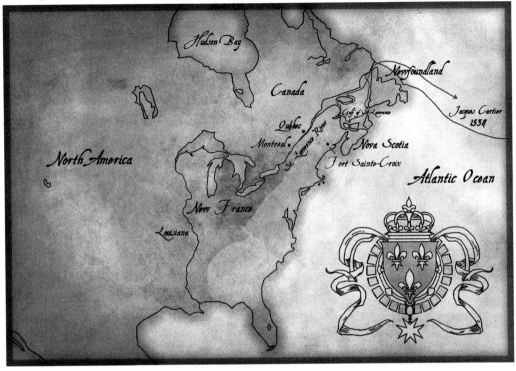

Samuel de Champlain explored the coast of Maine and Nova Scotia. He eventually established a settlement that became Quebec City.

In 1603, Champlain sailed to New France for the first time. He explored the coast of Maine and Nova Scotia. He founded his first settlement in Nova Scotia. In 1608, Champlain moved the settlement to the site of Quebec City, on the banks of the St. Lawrence River. At a point where the river narrows, Champlain built a town on the heights with a view of the river.

New France grew differently than the English colonies. At first very few settlers came to New France. The winters were long and hard. Farming was difficult because the **growing season** was so short.

Vocabulary

growing season, n. the days available in a year to plant and harvest crops

Those who did settle in New France were mostly rugged adventurers. For a while that suited the French government. The colony made a profit, and for the most part the colony's few settlers did not need a great deal of supervision.

It is probably true to say that the settlers in New France also dealt with the Native Americans living nearby somewhat differently than the English did in the colonies to the south. English colonists forcefully pushed Native Americans off land they had lived on for generations. In New France, the relationship between the fur traders and the Native American tribes was more peaceful. The French had not tried to conquer the Native Americans, but instead had focused on trade.

The fur trade also resulted in further exploration. Fur traders canoed and **portaged** farther and farther into the North American wilderness. In 1673, an expedition led by Jacques Marquette

> **Vocabulary**
> ....
> **portage,** v. to carry boats and supplies overland from one waterway to another

(/mahr*ket/) and Louis Jolliet (/joe*lee*ae/) became the first European expedition to reach the Mississippi River.

The Mississippi River

In 1682, a French explorer with the imposing name of René-Robert Cavelier, Sieur de La Salle (/reh*nae/roh*bayr/kah*vel*yae/syer/duh/lah/sal/) sailed down the Mississippi River to the Gulf of Mexico. La Salle claimed all the land drained by the Mississippi for the king of France.

By 1700, New France was a sizable empire with hardly any settlers. There were only about ten thousand Europeans in the entire area. The fur trade was profitable, true. But if a competitor appeared, France would have a hard time defending its lands. And that competitor was right next door. England and France were rivals in Europe. They would soon become rivals in North America as well.

Chapter 9
Dutch Trade

Control of the Spice Trade

For many years, the Portuguese controlled the spice trade from the Cape of Good Hope to the most distant shores of the Indian Ocean.

The Big Question
....
How did the death of a king affect the Spice Trade?

They had settlements up and down the African coast and a main trade center at Goa, on the west coast of India.

Spain was growing wealthy by mining the gold that had been discovered in the Americas. It did not become especially interested in the spice trade until the death of a particular king.

In 1580, King Henry of Portugal died. His death changed the history of the spice trade. A king's death could create political unrest when it was unclear who should succeed him. That's what happened in Portugal. Henry had no adult son to take over the throne. Seven different people presented themselves as having the right to be the next king of Portugal. One of them was King Philip II of Spain. Philip was related to Henry on his mother's side. After some conflict, Portugal and Spain were brought together under the rule of the Spanish King Philip II.

After the death of Portugal's King Henry, King Phillip II of Spain became ruler of both Spain and Portugal.

At first there was little effect on the spice trade. The Spanish navy was the most powerful in the world. It could protect Portuguese ships sailing to Asia. Only now a good part of the profits went to the king of Spain.

In 1588, the defeat of the Spanish Armada tipped the balance of sea power in the world. The defeat crippled Spain as a sea power. At the time, Spain was at war with the Dutch. As Spanish power declined, the Dutch saw an opportunity for their country, the Netherlands, to take control of the spice trade.

The Dutch were excellent sailors and merchants, and they had a developing interest in the spice trade. A Dutch seaman named Jan van Linschoten (/yahn/vahn/lihn*skoe*tun/) played an important role. As a sailor, Linschoten spent his life looking for a northeastern route to the Spice Islands, a route that did not exist. When he stopped exploring, Linschoten worked in India, keeping long and detailed notes about the Eastern traders he worked with. The information he gathered was a great help to the Dutch as they entered the spice trade.

The Dutch set up their main trade center on the island of Java in present-day Indonesia. They named the community Batavia. (Today it is called Jakarta and is the capital city of Indonesia.) It was far away from the Portuguese on the African coast but close to the nutmeg, mace, and cloves found in the Spice Islands.

In the early 1600s, Dutch merchants formed a joint-stock company called the Dutch East India Company. The company received a **charter** from the government

> **Vocabulary**
> ....
> **charter,** n. a document issued by an authority giving a group certain rights

giving it a monopoly on all trade stretching east from the Cape of Good Hope in Africa to the Straits of Magellan in South America. Dutch power and control of the spice trade grew.

Because the Netherlands is a very small country without many resources of its own, the Dutch did not have many goods to trade from their home ports. Instead, they traveled throughout the East gathering up goods to trade. Dutch ships called at ports all over Africa, India, and other Asian countries. They voyaged into the Persian Gulf and all the way to Japan. They traded silver from one place for cloth or tea from another. The trades were set up so that, in the end, spices ended up in the hands of the Dutch for transport to Europe.

The Dutch worked hard to control the amount of spices available in Europe. For example, if there was too much of one spice available, they would destroy supplies of it to prevent the price of that spice from falling. Since the trading center at Java was so

The Dutch developed a trade empire that stretched from Europe across Asia to Japan.

far away from the Netherlands, the Dutch East India Company got permission to set up a government of its own. Company leaders had their own army, minted their own money, and created their own laws to keep everyone in line.

A Stopover Colony

Traveling from Java to the Netherlands took a very long time. The Dutch needed a rest stop along the way. They found a location for just such a stop, largely by accident. A storm-damaged Dutch ship managed to limp into Table Bay on the southern tip of Africa, where it sank. The surviving sailors found that Table Bay had everything needed for a supply station, including a good harbor and a fair climate. In 1657, the Dutch founded the colony of Cape Town there. The colony soon became a major settlement.

Over the years, many Dutch explorers set out across the Pacific to find new trade centers. Sailing from southeast Java, Dirk Hartog came upon Australia. In 1643, Abel Tasman landed on the island now named Tasmania, off Australia's southeastern coast. By sailing around Australia, Tasman proved that it was a huge island unconnected to any other land.

For two hundred years, through the 1600s and 1700s, the Dutch profited from the spice trade in Asia.

Henry Hudson

As you have learned, countries involved in the spice trade were eager to find a quicker way to reach Asia from northern Europe. In 1609, the Dutch East India Company hired an English explorer named Henry Hudson. Hudson wanted to be the explorer who found the Northwest Passage that everyone was seeking.

Hudson took a small crew on a small ship called the *Half Moon*. He sailed north, following the coast of Norway. The farther north the *Half Moon* traveled, the colder and icier it got. The crew began to grumble. Conditions on the ship went from bad to worse. Hudson had planned to find a passage that would take him over the North Pole and down to the Malay Archipelago. Instead, he changed his mind and headed west.

Hudson charted the *Half Moon's* course down the Atlantic coast of North America to find the Northwest Passage. At the mouth of what is now the Hudson River, he claimed land for the Netherlands.

For the first few days that the *Half Moon* sailed up the Hudson River, Hudson must have felt great excitement. The river was wide and deep, with steep sides and a strong current. Surely this was the passage through the continent. Hudson sailed up the river to the site of present-day Albany, New York. But when the river grew shallow, it became clear that it would not lead to the Pacific Ocean. Hudson returned to Europe.

The next year, Hudson returned to North America, this time on an English ship, the *Discovery*. Hudson was sure he would have to sail north to find the Northwest Passage. He discovered a huge inland sea, which he mistook for the Pacific Ocean. Today that Canadian body of water is called Hudson Bay.

Hudson and his men quickly realized they were in an inland sea. Winter came rapidly. The ship got stuck in the ice, and food ran

Mutinous crew members forced Henry Hudson off his ship to face certain death in the cold and barren area.

low. The crew grew angry and mutinied. Hudson, his son, and some loyal sailors were forced off the ship and into a small boat. They were never heard from again. Sailors on the *Discovery* made it back to England. They were never punished for the mutiny.

New Netherland

Dutch merchants were eager to make money from the land claimed by Hudson. In 1614, a group of these merchants formed a joint-stock company called the New Netherland Company.

The company's first activity was fur trading. A trading post was built at Fort Orange (today, Albany, New York) far up the river explored by Hudson. The fur trading went well, and merchants prospered. But the company was unsuccessful in getting colonists to this new land. Most people in the Netherlands, a small country, were reluctant to leave their homeland to live in a distant wilderness.

Eventually a new company called the Dutch West India Company took over. In 1626, Peter Minuit (/mihn*yoo*iht/), the head of the Dutch West India Company, came to the island of Manhattan and acquired the island from the Native Americans. Today, the island of Manhattan is the heart of New York City. On the southern tip of Manhattan, the Dutch built a town they called New Amsterdam. The town grew, but slowly.

The Dutch government didn't think New Amsterdam was worth the high cost of defending it. In 1664 an English warship sailed into New York Harbor and took over the colony. The English renamed the colony New York in honor of the duke of York. The Dutch efforts to colonize North America were over.

The English easily captured the Dutch colony of New Amsterdam. They renamed the colony New York.

Chapter 10
Slavery

Age-Old Practice There had been enslaved people for many years prior to the Age of Exploration. For centuries people throughout the world had enslaved those they had conquered. But Europeans used their power and wealth to spread the practice of slavery on a vast scale. In doing so, they dramatically changed the lives of millions of people.

The Big Question

How did the Age of Exploration lead to the development of the slave trade?

Slavery was part of African life long before Europeans arrived. Muslim states in North Africa marched Africans across the Sahara to markets in the Middle East. Traders also shipped people from East Africa across the Indian Ocean to sell them into slavery. Many African cultures also practiced slavery among themselves. But among some groups, enslaved people had rights. For example, in the Ashanti kingdom of West Africa, enslaved people could own property and marry, and they got their freedom after working for a set amount of time. Most importantly, children born to Ashanti-enslaved people were not automatically also enslaved.

Enslaved people were forced to work extremely hard in challenging conditions.

European involvement in the African slave trade began to grow after the year 1415 when the Portuguese seized the city of Ceuta (/she*yoo*tuh/) on the North African coast. During the next hundred years, nearly two hundred thousand Africans were taken to become enslaved workers in parts of Europe, and to islands in the Atlantic.

In the 1400s, Portuguese and Spanish explorers discovered several groups of islands in the Atlantic Ocean. Colonists quickly settled on these islands. Portugal built colonies on Madeira (/muh*deer*uh/), São Tomé (/sou/tuh*meh/), and the Azores (/ae*zorz/). Spain colonized the Canary Islands.

Spanish and Portuguese colonists realized that the land and climate in these islands would be good for growing the cash crop sugar, which was in high demand in Europe. In order for growing sugar to be a profitable business, though, huge fields of sugarcane had to be planted and harvested. This required lots of workers. For Spanish and Portuguese plantation owners, large numbers of enslaved people provided the needed labor. As sugar plantations sprang up, the demand for enslaved workers grew.

Slavery in the Americas

After Columbus came upon the islands of the Caribbean Sea, the Spanish quickly colonized the region. Spanish colonies throughout the Americas were established to benefit Spain. In Mexico and Peru, the Spanish gathered vast amounts of gold and silver. They used indigenous people to work in the mines.

The islands of the Caribbean were not rich in mineral wealth. The land and climate, however, were well-suited for growing sugar and other crops. Experts from the Canary Islands came to Hispaniola and other islands to help the Spanish set up sugar plantations. These plantations needed an inexpensive labor force. At first, plantation owners planned to use local people to work on the plantations. But disease and war, which had largely been brought to the islands by the Europeans, killed many indigenous people.

As had been the case in the Azores and the Canary Islands, enslaved people from Africa provided a **cost-effective** answer. However, this practice was incredibly **inhumane**, and caused much suffering. The Spanish were not the only Europeans who thought of this solution. Portuguese colonists found that sugar was well-suited to the coastal regions of Brazil. They imported people to use as enslaved labor to grow sugarcane there. In the 1600s, England colonized several islands in the Caribbean, including Jamaica and St. Kitts. British planters, too, turned to enslaved people from Africa to work on their sugar plantations. Sugar made the planters rich. But the sugar growers created another business that could make people rich—trading human beings across the Atlantic.

> ## Vocabulary
>
> **cost-effective,** adj. providing benefits without costing a great deal of money
>
> **inhumane,** adj. cruel, unacceptable

The Slave Trade

The Portuguese were the first Europeans involved in the Atlantic slave trade. Their explorations of the African coast had opened up new sources for people they could enslave. When Portugal's power collapsed and the Dutch took over the spice trade, they took over much of the Atlantic slave trade as well.

In 1619, a Dutch ship sailed into the mouth of the James River in the English colony of Virginia in North America and dropped anchor. On board were Dutch pirates who had been attacking other ships on the high seas. They had captured a shipload of enslaved Africans from a Spanish vessel heading for the Caribbean. Now the Dutch sailors were traveling north and needed supplies. The pirates traded these people for food. This was the first arrival of Africans in the English North American colonies. Whether these Africans became indentured servants or enslaved workers remains unclear.

One of the trade centers the Dutch had taken from the Portuguese was Elmina on the west coast of Africa (in present-day Ghana). For years, Elmina had been a Portuguese trade center where ivory

Captured Africans were held in Elmina Castle on the West African coast before being transported to Europe or the Americas.

and gold were exchanged. As the slave trade increased, Elmina became one of the forts where captured Africans were imprisoned before being transported to Europe or to the Americas. Before long, Elmina was the center of the Dutch slave trade.

By 1655, the Dutch were transporting 2,500 enslaved people across the Atlantic each year. When England seized control of New Netherland, there were five hundred Dutch-speaking Africans in the colony.

The slave trade was one side of a trading triangle. One segment of the triangle carried goods from Europe to Africa. Ships carried items such as iron, guns, gunpowder, knives, cloth, and beads. Another segment transported people from Africa to the Caribbean islands and later to the English colonies in North America.

Trade Triangle

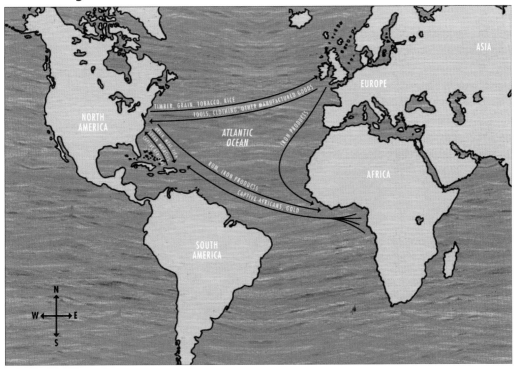

The slave trade was an important leg of the triangular trade that developed among Europe, Africa, and the Americas.

And another segment of the triangle made a return trip to Europe. These ships carried timber, tobacco, grain, sugar, and rice from the plantations of the Americas.

Middle Passage

Africans typically passed through several stages in their journey into slavery. First, they were captured, sometimes by European slavers but usually during wars among African tribes. Next they were marched to a seaport such as Elmina. There they were packed into ships for the journey across the Atlantic. Those who survived the journey were sold at the slave market in a seaport in the Americas and transported to plantations.

The trip across the Atlantic Ocean was known as the Middle Passage. It was a terrible, dehumanizing experience. Slave

The Middle Passage was a harsh experience that many did not survive.

ships usually carried between 150 and six hundred Africans. Enslaved people were treated like **cargo**, not people. They were chained on platforms. Each person had a space about six feet long and

Vocabulary

cargo, n. goods transported by a ship, plane, or truck

sixteen inches wide. Because they were chained in place, they could not even turn over.

As the ships passed through tropical latitudes, temperatures in the hold would rise to over one hundred degrees. Enslaved people were fed small amounts of rice and water twice a day.

The trip across the ocean took between two and four months depending on the weather and the destination. Illness and death were common occurrences. With people packed in close quarters, disease spread easily. Historians estimate that about fifteen percent of enslaved people did not survive the journey. The Atlantic slave trade lasted nearly three hundred years. In that time, European slave traders made approximately fifty-four thousand voyages across the Atlantic.

The Growth of Slavery in the Colonies

In the colonies of North America, the demand for enslaved people came later in the slave trade. The Pilgrims and Puritans settled the colonies in the Northeast where the soil was not very good and the winters were cold. These conditions were not ideal for growing cash crops, so there was no need for a large labor force. Even so, slavery did exist on a small scale in these northern colonies.

In the South, the situation was different. Plantation owners who lived in the southern colonies grew tobacco to **export** to Europe. They needed many workers to run these plantations. To find a supply of workers, plantation owners began paying for **indentured servants** to come to the colonies from Europe. In return, the servants agreed to work for a certain number of years. A steady supply of workers could be brought from the home country, but it didn't work out very well.

Vocabulary

export, v. to send goods to sell in another country

indentured servant, n. a person who owes an employer a certain amount of work for a certain amount of time in exchange for some benefit

It was hard to keep the workers alive. The hot weather, high humidity, and swampy water were perfect conditions for breeding disease. Even those indentured servants who became accustomed to the new climate did not live very long. The work was very hard, and the conditions were very bad. Many servants did not survive long enough to fulfill their contracts. It was necessary to keep paying for servants to cross the ocean.

Despite these problems, when the plantations first got started, the owners were glad to pay for indentured servants instead of enslaved people. At the end of a certain amount of time, they were granted their freedom.

In time, the use of indentured servants became less attractive to the plantation owners. Little by little, the plantations moved away from the coast, where disease had been a big problem. Servants were living longer. They ate better and could avoid bad drinking water. Healthy servants started living long enough to fulfill their contracts. Plantation owners started having to pay out more in "freedom dues."

Freedom dues were what a servant received for completing his or her contract. According to the contract, an indentured servant was given food, clothing, money, and some livestock. Those who were given land could finish their contracts and start farming next door.

Before long, buying an enslaved workforce from Africa became more profitable and efficient than hiring indentured servants. Slavery spread in the 1700s. Millions of acres were planted with tobacco. Planters also introduced a new cash crop, rice, which needed lots of labor to plant and harvest.

In the late 1700s and 1800s, cotton became a third cash crop grown in the American South. Indigo and cotton **cultivation** also relied on the labor of enslaved people.

> **Vocabulary**
>
> **cultivation,** n. the planting, growing, and harvesting of crops

Plantation Life

The life of an enslaved person was very hard. People were sold as slaves at a market where owners bid against each other. Slaveholders bought the people they thought would work best for them. Families were frequently broken up; children were separated from their parents, and husbands from wives.

On the plantation, enslaved people had no freedom. They had to do what their masters told them to do and could not travel

Slaveholders sometimes separated children from their parents.

anywhere without permission. They could not testify in court, so an owner could mistreat an enslaved person and get away with it. Many colonies also had laws that made it illegal to teach enslaved people to read or write.

Enslaved people worked from dawn to nightfall, with an hour off midday in the heat. The work was hard. They worked in the cotton, rice, indigo, and tobacco fields. They chopped wood, built fences, cleared roads, and dug wells. All the while, they were watched by a person called an **overseer**. Other enslaved people worked in the master's house, performing tasks such as cooking and cleaning.

> **Vocabulary**
>
> **overseer,** n. someone who supervises workers to make sure a job is done properly

Not all Africans in the colonies were enslaved. Some managed to gain their freedom. A few slaveholders even gave freedom to their enslaved workers. Free Africans in the colonies made their living as farmers and crafts workers. After the American Revolution, slavery was abolished in most of the northern states. But slavery spread in the American South, where it survived until the end of the Civil War in the mid-nineteenth century.

Summing Up the Age of Exploration

The Age of Exploration brought tremendous changes to the world. The United States and Canada had their first beginnings in this era. They might not exist if the explorers you have learned about had stayed at home.

To have a full and well-balanced understanding of the Age of Exploration, we have to recognize that this age, like most ages, was better for some people than for others. Some people made their fortunes; others did not survive perilous journeys.

But for many people, the Age of Exploration was a time of great hardship. Contact with Europeans devastated the indigenous peoples of the Americas. Many died in battle, and disease killed millions more. For millions of Africans, contact with Europeans meant a lifetime of slavery. The image of a ship sailing proudly across the Atlantic becomes much less inspiring when we remember that many of these ships carried human cargo in inhumane conditions. An understanding of the age must include both the heroism of the explorers and the tragedies that resulted from exploration.

Exploration and Empires (ca. 1700)

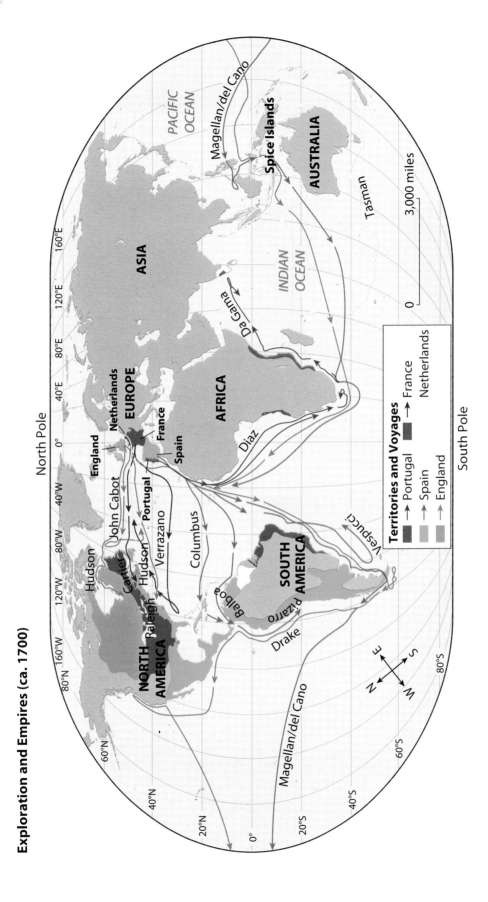

Glossary

A

archipelago, n. a chain of islands (4)

armada, n. a large fleet of ships (60)

astrolabe, n. a navigational tool used to determine the position of the sun, a star, or other object in the sky (15)

C

cargo, n. goods transported by a ship, plane, or truck (89)

cartographer, n. a mapmaker (66)

cash crop, n. a crop that is grown to be sold (44)

charter, n. a document issued by an authority giving a group certain rights (76)

circumnavigate, v. to travel completely around something (such as Earth), especially by water (53)

colonization, n. the practice of bringing people from a different country to control and settle an area that already has an indigenous population (57)

conquistador, n. the Spanish word for conqueror (44)

cost-effective, adj. providing benefits without costing a great deal of money (85)

cultivation, n. the planting, growing, and harvesting of crops (91)

cure, v. to preserve meat, fish, or other food by smoking, drying, or salting it (12)

D

diplomat, n. someone who represents the government of one country in another country (38)

"diplomatic mission," (phrase) a group of people who serve as representatives of their government in another country (8)

E

empire, n. a group of countries or territories under the control of one government or ruler (45)

expedition, n. a special journey taken by a group that has a clear purpose or goal (20)

exploitation, n. the practice of taking unfair advantage of a person or group (47)

export, v. to send goods to sell in another country (90)

F

fishery, n. an area of water where fish or other sea creatures are raised and caught (64)

fleet, n. a group of ships sailing together with the same purpose and under the control of the same leader (21)

G

growing season, n. the days available in a year to plant and harvest crops (71)

H

hourglass, n. a glass device that measures time using the flow of sand (17)

hull, n. the sides and bottom of a boat (14)

I

immunity, n. a body's ability to remain free of illness even after being exposed to the cause of the illness (42)

indentured servant, n. a person who owes an employer a certain amount of work for a certain amount of time in exchange for some benefit (90)

indigenous, adj. native to a particular region or environment (38)

inhumane, adj. cruel, unacceptable (85)

interpreter, n. a person who translates from one language to another (21)

iron ore, n. rock from which iron can be obtained (25)

isthmus, n. a narrow piece of land that connects two larger land masses (44)

J

joint-stock company, n. a company that raises money by selling shares, or interest in the company, in the form of stock (62)

L

landfall, n. the reaching of land, after a trip by sea (21)

league, n. a unit of distance equal to approximately three miles (33)

log, n. a written record of a ship's progress (33)

loot, v. to steal or take something by force (58)

M

magnetic compass, n. a device that uses a magnetized pointer to show direction (16)

medieval, adj. relating to the Middle Ages in Europe (2)

merchant, n. a person who buys and sells goods to earn money (7)

Mongol, n. a native of the Asian nation of Mongolia (8)

monopoly, n. a situation in which one person, country, or company has complete control of the supply of a good or service (6)

Moor, n. a North African follower of Islam during the Middle Ages (21)

motive, n. the reason for taking a specific action (10)

mutiny, n. the rebellion of a ship's crew against the captain (34)

N

navigation, n. the act of planning and directing the movement of a ship, plane, or other vehicle (14)

navigational, adj. related to controlling the movement of a ship (6)

negotiate, v. to discuss the terms of an agreement (7)

Northwest Passage, n. a sea route connecting the Atlantic Ocean and Pacific Ocean along the northern coast of North America (57)

O

overseer, n. someone who supervises workers to make sure a job is done properly (93)

P

plantation, n. a large farm where one or more crops were grown by a large number of laborers; these crops were sold for a profit by the plantation owner (44)

porcelain, n. a type of fine pottery (8)

portage, v. to carry boats and supplies overland from one waterway to another (72)

R

rain shadow, n. an area that gets less rain because it is on the protected side of a mountain (5)

rig, v. to prepare for sailing (15)

royal standard, n. a flag that represents a king or queen (35)

S

scurvy, n. a disease caused by a lack of vitamin C (24)

sextant, n. a navigational instrument that uses a telescope and scale to determine latitude and longitude (15)

spice, n. a plant used to add flavor to food (2)

strait, n. a narrow body of water that connects two larger bodies of water (50)

T

trade wind, n. a wind that almost always blows in a particular direction (24)

trader, n. a person who buys and sells goods (6)

trading center, n. a place where people buy and sell goods (6)

U

uncharted, adj. never mapped (14)

CKHG™
Core Knowledge HISTORY AND GEOGRAPHY™

Series Editor-In-Chief
E.D. Hirsch, Jr.

Subject Matter Expert

J. Chris Arndt, PhD, Department of History, James Madison University

Illustration and Photo Credits

Age Fotostock/SuperStock: i, iii, 19

Album/Oronoz/SuperStock: 9

Angela Padron: Cover D, 54–55

Brittany Tingey: 40

Christopher Columbus's Santa Maria/Private Collection/© Look and Learn/Bridgeman Images: Cover E, 32

Classic Vision/Age Fotostock/SuperStock: 67

Cover of "Short Account of the Destruction of the Indies" 1552 by Friar Bartolome de las Casas (1474–1566)/Photo © Tarker/Bridgeman Images: 47

Daniel Hughes: 58

Durga Bernhard: Cover C, 83, 88, 92

Dustin Mackay: 30–31, 34, 37, 42–43

Erika Baird: 71

Ferdinand Magellan (1480–1521)/Pictures from History/Bridgeman Images: 49

Galleon in full sail en route to Portugal, illustrated by the Coler (or Keller) family of Nuremburg (vellum), German School, (16th century)/British Library, London, UK/© British Library Board. All Rights Reserved/Bridgeman Images: 20

Jacques Cartier (1491–1557) Discovering the St. Lawrence River in 1535, 1847 (oil on canvas) by Jean Antoine Theodore Gudin (1802–80)/Château de Versailles, France/Bridgeman Images: 69

James Johnson: 46

Japan: Dejima Island, with Dutch flag flying. Chromolithograph of a painting by Johan Maurits (1807–1874)./Pictures from History/Bridgeman Images: 77

John Cardasis/SuperStock: 67

King Philip II of Spain by Albert Kretschmer (1825–91)/Private Collection/© Look and Learn/Bridgeman Images: 75

Map tracing Magellan's world voyage, once owned by Charles V, 1545 (vellum) by Battista Agnese (1514–64)/John Carter Brown Library, Brown University, RI, USA/Bridgeman Images: 53

Marco Polo at the court of Kublai Khan by Angus McBride (1931–2007)/Private Collection/© Look and Learn/Bridgeman Images: 8

Marti Major: 16, 56

Michael Parker: Cover A

Mutiny on board the fleet of Magellan by Tancredi Scarpelli (1866–1937)/Private Collection/© Look and Learn/Bridgeman Images: 50

Navigators using an astrolabe in the Indian Ocean, from the 'Livre des Merveilles du Monde', c.1410–12 (tempera on vellum) Ms Fr 2810 f.188, by the workshop of The Boucicaut Master, (fl.1390–1430)/Bibliotheque Nationale, Paris, France/Bridgeman Images: 7

Pepper harvest and offering the fruits to a king, from the 'Livre des Merveilles du Monde', c.1410–12 (tempera on vellum) Ms Fr 2810 f.186, by the workshop of The Boucicaut Master, (fl.1390–1430)/Bibliotheque Nationale, Paris, France/Archives Charmet/Bridgeman Images: 10–11

Photononstop/SuperStock: 12

Portuguese caravels, illustration from Memory of Armadas that from Portugal passed to India, Ms 1551, 16th century/Academia das Ciencias de Lisboa, Lisbon, Portugal/De Agostini Picture Library/G. Dagli Orti/Bridgeman Images: 1, 14

Scott Hammond: 80

Sharae Peterson: 63, 81

Shari Darley Griffiths: 45

Signing of Treaty of Tordesillas between Spain and Portugal, June 7, 1494/De Agostini Picture Library/G. Dagli Orti/Bridgeman Images: 39

Sir Francis Drake (1540–96) (gouache on paper) by Peter Jackson (1922–2003)/Private Collection/© Look and Learn/Bridgeman Images: 60

Sir Francis Drake's The Golden Hind/Private Collection/© Look and Learn/Bridgeman Images: 61

The Discovery of the Strait of Magellan (coloured engraving) by Oswald Walters Brierly (1817–94)/Private Collection/Index/Bridgeman Images: 52

The Voyage of Columbus, illustration after Arthur Michael (d. 1945) from 'This Country of Ours, The Story of the United States' by H.E. Marshall, 1917/Private Collection/The Stapleton Collection/Bridgeman Images: 33

Vasco da Gama lands at Kozhikode (Calicut, India), May 20, 1498/Pictures from History/Bridgeman Images: 25

Wolfgang Kaehler/SuperStock: 86

Yadid Levy/Robertharding/SuperStock: Cover B, 2–3